The Quest for Boundaries

Honoring Limits, yours and Others

Marsha Ferrick Heiden, PhD, BCC

i

The Quest for Boundaries

Honoring Limits, yours and Others

Marsha Ferrick Heiden, PhD, BCC

THE QUEST FOR BOUNDARIES

HONORING LIMITS, YOURS AND OTHERS

Written by Marsha Ferrick Heiden, PhD., BCC

Art by Marie Billings Dalton

Copyright 2016

Marsha Ferrick Heiden, PhD, BCC

PO Box 7515

Cave Creek, AZ 85327-7515

http://www.amaraquest.com

To

Gina

FOR INFORMATION AND AVAILABILITY FOR

SPEAKING ENGAGEMENTS, GROUP PROGRAMS, AND INDIVIDUAL MASTERY COACHING

PLEASE CONTACT THE AUTHOR DIRECTLY AT

marsha.heiden@gmail.com

VISIT

www.amaraquest.com

Additional Titles

www.amazon.com

Contents

Your Name

Date

What is a Boundary?

bound·a·ry[1]

ˈbound(ə)rē

noun

plural noun: boundaries

a line that marks the limits of an area; a dividing line.

"the eastern boundary of the wilderness"

a limit of a subject or sphere of activity.

"a community without class or political boundaries"

In general boundaries separate one thing from another. Boundaries can be very clear such as a fence or wall, or they can be far more nebulous without a clear beginning or ending. Personal boundaries are the latter, differing greatly between individuals, sub-cultures, and cultures.

---

[1] Google

List a few things that you can think of that have clear boundaries.

List a few things that have boundaries that are less clear, and harder to define.

Why are Boundaries Important?

Your personal boundaries protect the inner core

of your identity and your right to choices.

Gerard Manley Hopkins

It is important for you to have boundaries between yourself and the outside world. Boundaries are necessary for you to establish your own needs, ideas, opinions, and gifts. If your boundaries are too rigid, with no room for others to be near you emotionally you will become isolated. If your boundaries are too permeable, you can become so flexible that you forfeit your independent actions or opinions. The most difficult part of developing boundaries is to find a balance between boundaries that are too flexible or too rigid. Developing healthy boundaries is a major responsibility and a big step toward good self- care. As you develop increasingly better boundaries you will develop a better sense of the role you and others play. Your respect for yourself and others will grow. You will treat yourself and others with respect. You teach others to treat you with respect. You understand that you can control only yourself, your thoughts, and your actions, no one else's. You are responsible only for you. You are an owner of your life not a victim. You find flexibility in your boundaries. You respect that others are responsible for themselves. You gain clarity on your rights and those of others. You learn to respect other people's limits as well as your own. You listen more carefully to yourself and trust your intuition. You easily identify what hurts, what feels good, what is yours, and what is not. You learn what you are willing to lose, and what you have the courage to strive towards. Write about the importance of boundaries for yourself and of others in your life.

Types of Personal Boundaries

It is necessary, and even vital, to set standards

for your life and the people you allow in it.

Mandy Hale

There are five types of personal boundaries. They are physical, sexual, emotional, mental (intellectual), and spiritual.

Physical

Everyone has the right to say when, how, where and who touches or gets close to them. List three ways in which people do not allow others to physically violate their boundaries.

List ways in which you do not allow others to violate your physical boundaries.

List ways in which you do not violate the physical boundaries of others.

Emotional Boundaries

Everyone has the right to his or her own feelings. We are responsible for what we do with them and how we show them. Others are entitled to their own feelings and are accountable for their behavior. It is not our job to try to change or fix them. List three ways in which people do not allow others to emotionally violate their boundaries.

List ways in which you do not allow others to violate your emotional boundaries.

List ways in which you do not violate the emotional boundaries of others.

Intellectual Boundaries

Everyone has the right to his or her own thoughts. It is our choice to accept or reject what others say about what we think or say. To allow others, and ourselves to have the right of our own thoughts, and the communication of them, empowers us to begin to make our own choices about how we think. We allow others their own thoughts without interruption or ridicule. Owning our intellect is part of our growth. List three ways in which people do not allow others to intellectually violate their boundaries.

List ways in which you do not allow others to violate your intellectual boundaries.

List ways in which you do not violate the intellectual boundaries of others.

Sexual Boundaries

Everyone has the right to say when, where, how, why and who touches the sexual part of their bodies. It is okay to own our gender and sexual orientations. It is okay to tell someone about a sexual boundary violation. No one deserves to be sexually violated. List three ways in which people do not allow others to violate their sexual boundaries.

List ways in which you do not allow others to violate your sexual boundaries.

List ways in which you do not violate the sexual boundaries of others.

Spiritual Boundaries

We exercise healthy spiritual boundaries when we allow others and ourselves to define God in ways that make sense for each of us. When we allow others and ourselves the right to our own feelings and thoughts about spiritual matters we become empowered. List three ways in which people do not allow other to spiritually violate their boundaries.

List ways in which you do not allow others to violate your spiritual boundaries.

List ways in which you do not violate the spiritual boundaries of others.

Raising Awareness

First learn the meaning of what you say, and then speak.

Epictetus

Check the boxes that apply to you. Notice if your boundaries differ with different people or in different situations.

Noticing

☐ I do not notice when someone else displays inappropriate boundaries.

☐ I am wary of someone who wants to get too close to me too soon. I notice whether someone I am beginning to relate to has similar values and opinions.

☐ I disregard others' opinions and values as "wrong", thereby trusting no one. Not letting anyone help me.

Do you manage your boundaries differently with different people or situations? If so, why?

Invasion

☐ I do not notice when someone invades your boundaries.

☐ I notice when someone is overly helpful, tries to make decisions for me, or does not consult me about time commitments. I let others know I make my own decisions.

☐ I do not allow people to help me or give me feedback, even though it is appropriate.

Do you manage your boundaries differently with different people or situations? If so, why?

Accepting

☐ I accept food, gifts, touch, and sex when I do not want to do so.

☐ I decide before accepting something whether I want to accept it. I do not ask whether the other person's feelings will be hurt if I refuse.

☐ I do not accept food, gifts, touch, sex, even when I want to.

Do you manage your boundaries differently with different people or situations? If so, why?

Touch

☐ I touch people without asking.

☐ I do not touch others without thinking about whether they have given me signals that it is okay.

☐ I do not touch others ever.

Do you manage your boundaries differently with different people or situations? If so, why?

☐ I take as much as I can for the sake of getting.

☐ I do not "test" a relationship by keeping track of how much is given me as a way of measuring love. I allow myself to receive when I want to.

☐ I am not willing to take anything from anyone.

Do you manage your boundaries differently with different people or situations? If so, why?

Generosity

☐ I give as much as I can give for the sake of giving.

☐ I do not give beyond what I can afford materially or emotionally because it makes me feel secure to think I have "sacrificed" for the other person. I give when it feels right for me to give.

☐ I do not give to others because I am preoccupied with myself.

Do you manage your boundaries differently with different people or situations? If so, why?

Advantage

☐ I allow people to take as much from me as they can from you.

☐ I am aware of when I am being taken advantage of and I am willing to confront the other person about it.

☐ I believe that everyone is out to take advantage of me.

Do you manage your boundaries differently with different people or situations? If so, why?

Decision Making

☐ I let others direct my life.

☐ I know what I want from life and have goals in many areas. I listen to opinions but make the decisions for myself.

☐ I do not listen to other's opinions or points of view.

Do you manage your boundaries differently with different people or situations? If so, why?

Reality

☐ I let others describe my reality.

☐ I assume that my perception of what is going on is just as accurate as my partner's. I refuse to allow my partner to tell me, "You don't feel that way." I trust my own feelings and thoughts.

☐ I am not willing to listen as others describe their reality.

Do you manage your boundaries differently with different people or situations? If so, why?

Compartmentalizing

☐ I become overwhelmed by a person or preoccupied with a person.

☐ When I am in a relationship, I am able to "compartmentalize" other areas of my life and to continue to function in them.

☐ I do not allow myself to even think about another person that I'm interested in.

Do you manage your boundaries differently with different people or situations? If so, why?

Impulses

- [ ] I act on my first sexual impulse.

- [ ] My feelings and my self- esteem decide whether I act on sexual impulses. "Will I feel good about myself?" is my first question.

- [ ] I do not allow myself to be sexually excited or aroused even when I feel good about the person. I do not allow myself to act on these feelings even when I believe the timing is right.

Do you manage your boundaries differently with different people or situations? If so, why?

Sexuality

☐ I am sexual for my partner not self.

☐ I do not "fake" sexual feelings. I do not have sex to avoid hurting my partner's feelings. I cannot be nagged or blackmailed emotionally into having sex. I can have sex when I choose to.

☐ I do not have sex even for myself.

Do you manage your boundaries differently with different people or situations? If so, why?

Pleasing

☐ I go against my personal values or rights to please others.

☐ I have values which are not negotiable in a relationship, I am not willing to "do anything" for a partner.

☐ I refuse to do or say things that please me.

Do you manage your boundaries differently with different people or situations? If so, why?

Self-Defining

☐ I let others define you.

☐ I know who I am. I am wary of partners who want me to be different.

☐ I do not allow myself to be influenced by others; not letting in new information.

Do you manage your boundaries differently with different people or situations? If so, why?

☐ I believe others can anticipate my needs.

☐ I do not expect others to read my mind about what is going on with me. I
tell them.

☐ I do not allow others to take care of me or attend to my needs.

Do you manage your boundaries differently with different people or situations? If so, why?

Need Fulfilment

☐ I expect others to fill my needs automatically.

☐ I do not expect others to put me first in everything we do together. I do not expect a partner to make me okay by being there. I expect there to be mutuality in relationships.

☐ I do not ask for what I need. I refuse to ask for something from another. I pretend I do not need.

Do you manage your boundaries differently with different people or situations? If so, why?

Support

☐ I fall apart so that someone will take care of you.

☐ I do not play games about how I feel to get sympathy or support. I ask directly for what I need.

☐ I hide my neediness, vulnerability, and fears.

Are there differences between people that you interact with? If so, why?

☐ I abuse myself by not attending and abusing my personal limits around things such as sex, physical activity, food, and or work.

☐ I respect myself as a person who is worthwhile. I believe I am in charge of my body and what others do to it. I take care of my body and my health as a part of my respect for me as a total person.

☐ I neglect myself and do, not provide for my needs.

Are there differences between people that you interact with? If so, why?

Insights

What insights did you garner about yourself, and how you manage boundaries in your life with others? Did patterns or themes appear? If so what were they? Are you good with setting boundaries in some areas? Unable to set boundaries in other areas? Do you have areas in your life where you have very rigid and inflexible boundaries?

Reflections

The boundary to what we can accept is the boundary to our freedom.

Tara Brach

Reflection is vital to change. If we do not examine our mistakes we are doomed to repeat them. Errors are valuable tools to learning. In learning through reflecting new ideas for moving forward and change in our lives appear. These ideas may help us and also help others. Role modeling better boundaries can assist everyone we encounter. Reflection also brings light to our successes, as well as where we need to grow and change. Reflection gives us perspective, and helps us develop the fine nuances of developing healthy relationships with ourselves and others.

What is one boundary you have recently set?

Can you remember how you felt before and after you set the boundary?

How were you called on to re-enforce it? If so, how did you do it?

What are the most difficult kinds of boundaries for you to set and enforce?

Where are you not being respected in your life?

With whom do you need to set boundaries?

Are you angry, whining, constantly complaining or upset about something? If so, where are you not setting a boundary?

What is preventing you from taking care of yourself?

What do you think will happen if you do?

What do you think will happen if you don't?

How do you feel when you are around people with too many rules, regulations and rigid boundaries?

How do you feel when you are around people that will do anything you suggest or agree with anything you say, or have limited, or no boundaries?

In the past, what have you been willing to lose for the sake of a particular relationship?

What are you willing to lose now?

What are you not willing to lose?

Setting Limits

Givers need to set limits because takers rarely do.

Rachel Wolchin

When you identify the need to set a limit with someone, do you set it clearly, preferably without anger, and in as few words as possible? If not how could you change your approach?

Do you try to simultaneously set a boundary (a limit) and take care of another person's feelings? If so, how can you stop caretaking other's feelings and set boundaries effectively?

Pay attention to your anger, rage, complaining, and whining. These are clues that you need to set boundaries. Where does this occur? What boundaries need to be set?

What will you do when people test the boundaries you set?

Where will you be tempted to not act in congruence with your boundaries? How will you ensure that you act in congruence with your boundaries?

Identify the people in your life who are happy to respect your boundaries?

Consider that you will not set boundaries until you are ready and no sooner. Where are you not ready to set boundaries? What is preventing you?

Who in your life can act as a support system as you strive to establish and enforce boundaries?

Boundaries in Practice

I encourage people to remember that "No" is a complete sentence.

Gavin de Becker

This exercise requires someone to assist you. This practice will determine your physical interpersonal boundaries and aid you in becoming aware of and respecting limits set by others.

Process

Stand facing the person that is assisting you. Stand 8-10 feet apart. Have the other person begin walking towards you. Ask them to stop when you first feel uncomfortable with the closeness. Then answer the following questions.

At what distance did you recognize your boundary?

How were you surprised by your boundary? Why?

47

Change roles and repeat the process. When you were the one varying the distance were you allowed to get closer than was comfortable for you? What was different for you this time? Why?

How did it feel to be allowed to enter someone else's space that was to close? Did you set a imit? How did you do so?

Repeat the exercises with a different person. At what distance did you recognize your boundary?

How were you surprised by your boundary? Why?

Change roles and repeat the process. When you were the one moving were you allowed closer to your partner than was comfortable for you?

How did it feel to be allowed to enter someone else's space that was to close? Did you set a l mit? How did you do so?

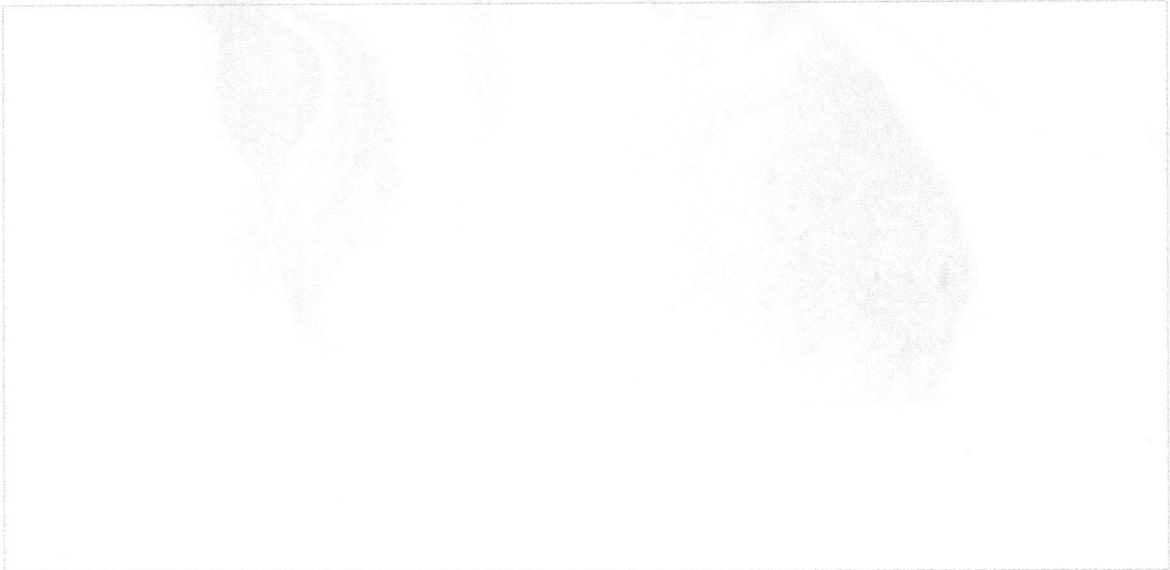

At what distance did you recognize your boundary?

How were you surprised by your boundary? Why?

Repeat the exercise and intentional alter the distance greater to smaller to greater. What was different for you this time? Why?

Change roles with your partner and repeat the process. When you were the one moving did your partner allow you to get closer than was comfortable for you? How did that feel? What did you do?

Do you feel more comfortable being close to someone of the same or opposite sex? Why or Why not?

Who are the people you allow to be close to you? Why?

What are the differences in your boundaries at work and at home?

Are your physical boundaries and emotional boundaries similar?

What insights do you have about boundaries and limits?

How do comfort zones in various cultures differ?

What differences in comfort zones might occur with same-sex partners versus opposite-sex partners?

Boundaries are based on life experiences, family and culturally learned rules, gender differences, and familiarity with the other person. What factors have shaped your boundaries? Are there other factors that have impacted your boundaries?

Consider if there may be places that you want to change how you manage your boundaries now that you have increased your awareness of them?

Creating Personal Space

Don't compromise yourself – you're all you have.

John Grisham

This exercise will help you develop a literal sense of your personal space and the location of your physical boundary. You will need two large pieces of paper to place on the floor to draw on and the assistance of another person.

Process

Put your paper on the floor. Stand in the center of your piece of paper. Have the other person do the same. Using a marker, draw what you believe is your personal space bubble around yourself. Explain your process? How do you feel?

Spend three to five minutes negotiating ways to make contact with each other physically while maintaining your own boundary. What feelings did you have when you made physical contact with the other person?

Next experiment with crossing your own boundary or the other person's boundary that is mapped on the floor. How did you feel when your own boundary was crossed?

How did you feel when you crossed your assistant's boundary?

Unacceptable Behavior

Dedicate yourself to building relationships on the

solid foundation of truth and authenticity.

Steve Maraboli

What unacceptable behavior do you tolerate? Consider the behaviors of others that you find uncomfortable to be around, perhaps even intolerable. Make a list of these behaviors. Be specific. Describe each situation and behavior in as much detail as you can.

Planning

Carefully consider each of the situations above, plan how will you respond in each situation. Take your time. How can you respond effectively with choice versus responding reactively without thought in each situation? Be specific. Rehearse each situation in your mind, along with your newly planned response.

Be specific. What boundaries will you tighten up?   Why?   How will you tighten your boundaries?

Be specific. What boundaries will you relax? Why? How will you do so?

What new boundaries will you set? Why? How will you do so?

How will you tell others? What will you say to them to let them know you will be setting new limits? Be certain to communicate clearly. Make direct requests. Offer them acceptable alternative(s) to their current behavior(s). Consider the following statements as an example, *"I want to eliminate (name behavior) from my life. When you (name behavior), I will (name your new behavior)."* Write a statement for each one of your new limits so that it is clear, direct, and offers an alternative.

No matter how well you set boundaries there will be individuals that do not respect your boundaries. People that repeatedly ignore clear boundary setting require special consideration. Why are they not respectful of your boundaries? Age? Ability? Disrespect? Contempt? Malice? Children may require repeated limit setting given their age and developmental status. Some individuals may be limited by their intelligence or developmental ability and may also require greater tolerance and repeated reminders. However, individuals that are repeatedly disrespectful, contemptuous, or malicious must be avoided. If you must deal with someone like this limit the time you spend with them, and do not give them an inch. If possible, have a supportive person with you. It is important to remember that you do not have to tolerate anyone's bad behavior, and you may *walk away* at any time. Where will you draw the line in the sand? Be specific.

Treasure

Trust that it is more important to fulfill your authentic desires

than listen to your fears. Trust that your intuition is leading

you somewhere. Trust that the flow of life contains you,

is bigger than you, and will take care of you. If you let it.

Vironika Tugaleva

What have you learned on this Quest? What are you taking with you that will help on your continued life journey? Spend some time reflecting on the lessons you have learned. Write them down so that you may review them.

FOR INFORMATION AND AVAILABILITY FOR

SPEAKING ENGAGEMENTS, GROUP PROGRAMS, AND INDIVIDUAL MASTERY COACHING

PLEASE CONTACT THE AUTHOR DIRECTLY AT

marsha.heiden@gmail.com

VISIT

www.amaraquest.com

Additional Titles

www.amazon.com